Leaving Lumberton

Leaving Lumberton

Sheryl Slocum

RESOURCE *Publications* · Eugene, Oregon

LEAVING LUMBERTON

Copyright © 2022 Sheryl Slocum. All rights reserved. Except for brief quotations in critical publications or reviews, no part of this book may be reproduced in any manner without prior written permission from the publisher. Write: Permissions, Wipf and Stock Publishers, 199 W. 8th Ave., Suite 3, Eugene, OR 97401.

Resource Publications
An Imprint of Wipf and Stock Publishers
199 W. 8th Ave., Suite 3
Eugene, OR 97401

www.wipfandstock.com

PAPERBACK ISBN: 978-1-6667-5993-8
HARDCOVER ISBN: 978-1-6667-5994-5
EBOOK ISBN: 978-1-6667-5995-2

12/08/22

Sheryl Slocum, Gravel, was first published in *The Perch*, a creative arts journal of the Yale Program for Recovery and Community Health, a program of the Yale School of Medicine.

This book is dedicated in gratitude
to the Hartford Avenue Poets:
You are critics, coaches, cheerleaders, and friends.
What more could a poet want?

Contents

Honors, and
   Acknowledgements ix

STUMPS

I Watched the Devil
   Eat an Orange 3
Betrayed 5
The White Frame House by
   the Road 6
Sisyphus and His Boulder 7
His Rig 8
The Pair 9
Control 10
Exorcism at the
   Old Orphanage 11
Gravel 13
Refugees 14
Combat Veteran 16
Small Church 17
The Landfill 18
Winter Moon and Tree 19
Flood 20
Hurricane Mitch 21
Near Sauk City,
   Wisconsin 23
The Drowned 25
Frost 27
Cemeteries 29

TURNING

St. Paul's, K Street 33
At the Point 35
Crossroads 37
Suicide Bomber 38
At Soldier's Gunpoint 40
Crossing the Red Sea 41
After Evensong 42
Infant's Hands 43
First of Winter 44
Venus's Voyage 45
Upon Leaving a Daughter
   at College in Boston 46
Visiting Colonial Virginia 49
Alzheimer's Jonah 51
Fighting Fire 52
Farewelling Randy 53
Rebecca at the End 54
The Renaming of Jacob 56
The Great Vigil 57
Thomas Merton 59
The Wake 60
Thief in the Night 61
Repentance 62
Germination 63

Moving On

Above Lumberton with Judy	67
The Morada	69
At the River Crescent	71
Gravity	72
House Blessing	73
Attuned	74
Mardi Gras in Wisconsin	75
Cloudburst	76
Thaw	77
Persephone's Return	78
Just a Sprig of Lilac	79
Double in White	80
Eucharist in Ashland, Wisconsin	81
Minaret	83
Girl and Truck	84
Writer	85
When in Your Garden Poets Recite	86
Runner I	87
My Life as a Bullet	88
Runner II	90
Lone Skateboarder	91
Baltimore Oriole	92
Fountain	93
Hopscotch	94
Fly Fishing	95

Honors, and Acknowledgements

Honors received by poems in this volume:

- 2019 Honorable Mention, Wisconsin Fellowship of Poets Triad History Theme Contest: "Near Sauk City, Wisconsin"
- 2018 Sundress Best of the Net Anthology nomination: "My Life as a Bullet"
- 2017 Honorable Mention, Wisconsin Fellowship of Poets Triad Poet's Choice Contest, "Cemeteries"
- 2015 Pushcart Prize nomination: "At Soldier's Gunpoint"
- 2005 1st Prize: Wisconsin Academy of Sciences, Arts and Letters Poetry Contest: "Fly Fishing"
- 1999 Honorable Mention, Wisconsin Fellowship of Poets Trophy Poem Contest: "Near Sauk City, Wisconsin"
- 1997 Honorable Mention, *ByLine Magazine* Annual Literary Contest: "The Morada"
- 1996 1st Prize, *ByLine Magazine* Spring Poem Contest: "Just a Sprig of Lilac"

Grateful acknowledgement is made to the editors and publishers of magazines, anthologies, and websites where some of the poems in this collection originally appeared.

Alverno College's *Inside Out:* Infant's Hands (2007), Thaw (2004), Control (2003), Girl and Truck (2003), After Evensong (2002), Minaret (2003), The White Frame House by the Road (2001), Above Lumberton with Judy [published as Climbing with Judy] (1999)

An Ariel Anthology: Map Edition: Venus's Voyage [published as Plotting Venus's Voyages] (2018)

The Anglican Theological Review: Repentance (Fall 2018), The Great Vigil (Winter 2011), Attuned (Summer 2008), St. Paul's K Street, Washington, DC (Spring 2005), After Evensong (Winter 2004), Eucharist in Ashland, Wisconsin (Fall 2002), I Watched the Devil Eat an Orange (Summer 2000), Germination (Summer 1999)

Artery III [chapbook anthology]: Lone Skateboarder (2003)

Blueline: Flood (2016), Persephone's Return (2006), Just a Sprig of Lilac (2000)

BoomerLitMag [online]: Hopscotch (2020)

Bramble: My Life as a Bullet (Winter 2018)

Collateral [online]: Refugees (November 2017)

Comstock Review: The Drowned (Fall/Winter 2021)

Exit 13: Visiting Colonial Virginia (2015)

God's Acre: The Spirit of the Churchyard [anthology]: The Morada (2000)

Hard Shell online: The Pair [published in part as Her Mind] (Spring 2001)

Hodge Podge: Betrayed (Summer 1996)

Hummingbird: The Pair [published in part as The Wit] (Spring 2019)

Masquerades and Misdemeanors [anthology]: At the River Crescent; Fighting Fire (2013)

Medical Literary Messenger [online and hard copy]: Rebecca at the End (Fall/Winter 2016)

The Montserrat Review: Crossing the Red Sea (2001)

No, Achilles: War Poetry [anthology]: At Soldier's Gunpoint (2015)

100 Words: Winter Moon and Tree (1999)

The Perch, a creative arts journal of the Yale Program for Recovery and Community Health, a program of the Yale School of Medicine: Gravel (Fall 2017)

Poets to Come: A Poetry Anthology: When in Your Garden Poets Recite (2019)

The Raintown Review: Alzheimer's Jonah (1998)

Red River Review [online]: His Rig (2001)

Santa Fe Literary Review: Gravity (2018)

Wheaton Alumni Magazine: Thomas Merton (1988)

Wisconsin Academy Review: Fighting Fire (Spring 2005), Fly Fishing (Spring 2005), First of Winter (Winter 2004), Frost (Spring 2001)

The Wisconsin Poets' Calendar: The Wake (2013), Baltimore Oriole (2011), Cloudburst (2005)

A Wise Woman's Garden: Writer (1997)

Stumps

I Watched the Devil Eat an Orange

I watched the Devil eat an orange
        once.
First, he squeezed it, strong fingers
        testing.

It was ripe.

Then he poked his sharp-nailed
        thumb in—
sank it right up to the
        knuckle,

looking at me all the while.

He put both thumbs into the hole
        and ripped.
Offering half to me, he passed the other
        under his nose

and smiled.

Using his long, white teeth, his tongue
        and lips,
he separated torn sections from soft rind.
        Neatly,

completely, he ate it.

He nodded in my direction,
        dabbed juice
from his lips with a fine, white cloth.
        Then
he winked at me, waved,
        and

tossed the skin away.

Betrayed

How was I to know the message
you wrote with your pies was false?
I put my head down and drank in
their sweetness. "How truly I am loved!" I thought,
beguiled by the skill of your fingers.
Ox-like, I ate unquestioningly while you—
weaver of recipes—netted me in spun sugar.
Now, sick and loveless, I am no longer
tempted by your well-trimmed delights. I have no more
stomach for the craft of your ginger-cakes,
for the perfidy of your real-butter shortbread.

The White Frame House by the Road

Two-story white frame house
surrounded by trees—
white face peering
from between green curtains,
eyes open wide—
blindless windows looking, looking.
What do they see?

World hurrying by
hardly heeding the always-looking,
the always-waiting for someone
to come in and turn on the light.

Sisyphus and His Boulder

In this damnation, nothing wears down.
But I, yes, I have learned my lesson.
My curse's surface has become familiar:
its grittiness, its protrusions that gall,
the hollows where I must be sure of my hold.

No matter which way the slope tumbles it,
I know how to anticipate, how

to scramble, then wait, where

                   to brace my feet, to re-

                           direct downhill in-

                   to uphill, to lose the least a-

          mount of time, use the

least amount of energy.

I've paid my price.
I'm a reformed man.
Now I'm the one who's in control.

His Rig

Big, glistening treads of his truck tires
roll over and over:
coiled snakes,
coiled and ready to strike
like his fist
hard, fast,
diamond-shaped on his muscular arm,
his wife's and son's bruises
dark as Goodyear rubber.

The Pair

Her mind

is like a hairpin
sharp
scratching
scraping scalp as she moves in
for the clinch

good at stabbing ideas
clamping them tightly
till they conform
to the shape she wants

until they sit together
in a row
crimped
as prettily as curls

The Wit

His voice,
a pair of pliers,
twists words sharp.

We all laugh, afraid
of what steel pincers
make us forget.

Control

His *controll* is so tight
she must end the word
with an extra *l*
to clamp it down,
to bind the *o* close
so it can't wiggle.

Still, it rolls its eye at her.

She wishes she could put it out.
She wishes she could blind the eyes
of all the world
so no one would see
how she succumbs
to his control.

Exorcism at the Old Orphanage

The former dormitory regrets the souls,
        they say,
that languished and left traces
        they can sense,
so she follows them,
        young American poet
trailing four Australian Pentecostals
        whose intercessions sound like groans
dragged up through basement ducting.

The redheaded woman intones
        a continuous prayer
in an incomprehensible tongue;
        her tall, heavy husband
gabbles Bible verses
        in noisy Aussie English;
the others pray and weep
        as they pace the rooms,
pausing in corners or near windows
        where misery remnants
must be especially strong.

        To the poet-in-training
these had been almost just
        windows, almost
just pale, institutional walls.
        Yet, some soul's anguish

stirs, making her wonder
        about exorcists,
the way the tall, heavy one
        gobbles as he eats,
how loudly he talks,
        and how his redheaded wife
softly pronounces, "No-eh, No-eh,"
        when she means "No,"
almost like a moan.

Gravel

loose scrabble of stones
    only ice
    or moving water
could have made you
could have left you so
    fragmented

it took a river years
of rolling you around
    in its mouth
clattering you against
    its teeth
or maybe a lake
    slapping and slapping
and in winter its frozen edge
    grinding

now I step gingerly
not wanting to twist my ankle
    on your hard life
not wanting to fall
    have the shape of you
    gouged
        into my knees
    printed
        into the heels of my hands

Refugees

Forced to wander without
		language,
those memories leave
		footprints,
the kind that made
		you tremble
and hide, try to still
		the klaxon
thudding of your heart,
		stifle
the animal rasping in
		your throat.

Those silenced rhizomes
		shoot out runners
to snare and trip you at
		ordinary moments:
meat searing on a stove,
		an infant's cry,
a whiff of dank mud
		after rain.

You sleep with the light on,
		but still
the wordless ones fasten
		clammy fingers
around your throat.
		You wake,

gasping syllables of
    the tongue
you locked away, those
    expressions
your children will never know,
    those words
nobody here can understand.

    You refuse
to recognize them.

Combat Veteran

How does he live
    who braced so long
        for death?

How does he relax
    when each current of air
        hisses the approach
            of an unseeable enemy?

How does he believe
    while every cross
        is crosshairs on a steeple
            gliding to a fix
                on him?

Small Church

Too many prayers lie crumpled
        in the corners.
Their dust, fine and lavender,
        weights the air,
dampening the votive flames
        so they flicker
and sputter at the feet
        of the stone Pietà
bent over the form
        of her dead son.

The Landfill

Bulldozers comb and recomb
      the growing mound,
molding a new topography.
      Already, the earlier hill
towers lush and green
      awaiting the next
and the next, a constructed
      horizon. No
picnicking families, no
      barefoot children, no
lovers roam the cool grass.
      The green hill
broods, fenced off in tiers.
      White studs,
barely visible, belie
      the overgrown rubble
of a modern pyramid.
      And I, knowing
its origin, wonder about the forbidden,
      the sacred:
its flocks of carrion birds, its
      sickening-sweet effluvia
and methane decomposition, its
      loveliness taboo.

Winter Moon and Tree

Last night the full moon pushed
on the new tree in our back yard,
pushed and pinned tree shadow
to the shining, snowy ground.
Each branch and twig lay printed
as surely as if the tree had fallen,
its weight cutting swaths into downy white,
swaths that filled with liquid night.
The moon stopped pushing,
but the night kept coming
and swallowed the young tree
into thirsty dark.

Flood

The river shrugs
        its swollen cobra body
along its ditch
        through the center of town,
fondling basements
        of houses built too close,
sucking marrow
        from embankments
holding up our bridges.

The river has swallowed
        the low land;
reeds and willows shiver
        waist-deep in chill, still
sky reflections.

The river has slithered
        even into our bedrooms.
In our sleep we hear water;
        we wake in the dark, thirsty,
or is it the river's thirst we feel,
        flicking its tongue
into our dreams?

Hurricane Mitch

Eight looms stand
in the basement of our North American school,
eight partially assembled then forgotten looms,
derelict and tangled scaffolds
in the half light of an underground corridor
between two buildings.

I use the corridor when it storms.
Wind shouts down draft-holes,
whines and shivers
through interwoven pipes and heat ducts,
brushes leftover threads dangling
from the loom frames.

This time,
the basement has sprung a leak.
Water seeps from a crack,
trickles a slow, dirty stream
between the loom legs,
searches for downhill,
an easy path to the drain.

In Central America,
over ten thousand die.
Whole huts and houses wash
down twisting, frothing torrents;
entire villages vanish

under collapsing mountainsides.
Families huddle in the half dark,
listen to the shrieking wind;
bare feet sense a tremor;
husbands' and wives' eyes meet,
children whimper.

Next week, maybe,
someone will discover them,
an elbow out of the mud here,
a foot or hand there,
bodies in disarray,
like looms unstrung,
bobbins missing,
shuttles warped,
temples splintered,

buried in indifferent earth
by careless wind and
reckless, thoughtless water.

Near Sauk City, Wisconsin

Farmers crimp their orchards
into the lees of sudden hills
that once were flat lakebed

which sank and sank
until the sand melted glassy,
shiny as the bellies
of freshly dead fishes.

Then the earth folded, squeezed,
broke, twisted, and spewed it up
into jutting quartzite hills

where Black Hawk and his band of fifty
held off an army of one thousand
while the Sauk people flowed
like a slow river
to a few days' safety
before their blood soaked the ground.

Grass and trees hide
the hills' stony bones,
and the orchards bloom red blossoms,

but in fall and winter
their empty limbs hang
like fingers bent backward,

forced, sprained, deliberately
broken, bare of fruit
for hungry mouths in the earth.

The Drowned

Evening's glassy waves
wrestle melon sunset to shore,
the water's underside all shadow.

This is the time when lovers
emerge from dusty streets to stroll
barefoot along the line of pale foam
dividing sand from water,
when children leave their last romp,
farewells thin and piping in the quiet air.

Gulls bleat
and swallows chatter and dive
before yielding the sky to fluttering bats.
Moored catamarans and yachts
rock at anchor, a creaking
wood and metal ghost village.

And somewhere on the lake's stony bed
the body of today's drowned girl lies
with skulls and bones
of other lost swimmers.

Not in their world anymore,
the white quarter moon glides
blindly over the darkening lake
where I walk the strand and hear

each incoming wave as a sigh
for those who left these heavy waters
without a final look,
without a last goodbye.

Frost

Fields languish under striped sheets
       ridges white
       furrows dark

the first hard frost of the season
is as brittle as its name
      fr—o—st
      fr——st
cold slivers of sound

words, perhaps, from an earlier time
when names narrated:
      frrr!
breath between chattering teeth
      st!
thin ice breaking

maybe danger then was more immediate
      the speared, angry beast
      the sure festering of a wound

perhaps dying had less leisure
less of the—*ah*—
that grips *fr*—and—*st*
      lengthens their sound

less slow glazing over of mind and soul
that draws us repeatedly to bedsides
    bleaker than these fields

Cemeteries

are for the living;
the illusion of Elysian fields
shields us
from the brash vitality
of our lives.

Dismayed
at the absence
already shrinking,
we stand,

want,
ache
for somewhere sacred,

for granite,
grass, trees
to seize the terrible
forgetting,

make it wait.

Turning

St. Paul's, K Street

Washington, D.C.

cool dimness
after the glare and noise
of the street

brooding quiet magnifies
scrape of heel on stone
creak of kneeler
slide of garments
against undergarments

faint odor of tallow
reminiscent of crackling fat
immolated sacrifices
blood
slaughter

other odors too
wine
smoky incense
bayberry
clove

after praying alone
in the dusky sanctuary
a woman said
she had been accosted

sanctuary is a dangerous place
where a God of blood
scents your clothes and hair
and demands

from the flickering wick inside the hanging altar lamp
which of the five men you have lived with
was really your husband
and would you like a drink

At the Point

Wind and water
slap and slap the rocky shore.
Cottage owners
who can't afford bay docks
teeter from row boats
into larger craft
bobbing at anchor
in the green deep.

A woman
belly flops onto a deck,
the cacophony
of wind and wave
silencing her struggles to mime.

An elderly gentleman
reaches a long, pale leg
down toward his boat.
Thin shin gleams
in the dull light.
Finding no footing,
he pulls back,
reaches again,
seeks the boat floor
on the next swell.

From the footpath I watch,
firmly landed,
till I look up
to the racing chop of cloud.
Then the point
bucks and dips,
spray flies off
its saw-toothed prow,
earth reels,
and I stagger
on my way
past open lake
toward the bay's tame calm.

Crossroads

I could turn onto the country road at this intersection.

I could follow it as sun creeps up the flat, pale sky,
    pulling it into a dome.
I could watch harvesters crawl like bugs across fields
    of corn
mounding trucks so high with golden kernels they groan
    on their axles.
Summer's last insects could skate across my windshield . . .

I always leave a life behind at crossroads.

Suicide Bomber

Most intimate lover of
    my flesh,
I strap you next to
    my skin.
Your kiss will penetrate
    me
more deeply than any

husband, will ravish
    my virginity
more completely. You will know
    me
even more than
    my mother,
who will never lay out
    my limbs,
adjust my clothing, compose
    my face, hands
one last time. Somewhere, she weeps

while I prepare as for
    my wedding.
I should have henna for
    my hands,
its thin lines like wires netting
    my palms,
or my grandmother's blue
    garter,

    its embroidered casing rubbing
            my inner thigh.
There should be gifts, singing,

women's suggestive jokes,
            my warm cheeks.
Without my consent,
            my face
takes up a girl's smile;
            I feel
its feather touch at
            my lips
as I step into the street, toward
            our consummation.

At Soldier's Gunpoint

Click of metal
the guard taken off
or the hammer cocked
I did not know
that click was enough

Posed as if unafraid
I froze
waiting for my heart
to beat
or shatter

I wish I had looked him in the eye
had held him
at the point of my only weapon

Perhaps there were no bullets
I did not know
but I do know it did not matter

The moment was loaded
and I must wait
for it to pass

Crossing the Red Sea

The corn on either side of the dirt tracks
is higher than the hood of the pickup.
They pause while Uncle Tom and Dad talk
yields per acre and market prices.

Alone in the back, she hears the ominous rustle
of stern walls of corn—
great, green tidal waves,
brooding shadow at their base,
hissing froth on top.

The pillar of dust raised by the truck
hangs heavily behind them,
hiding, perhaps, a pursuing menace;
ahead, the chalky tracks disappear into towering stalks.
They are surrounded!

Fairly suffocating, she presses her fear
flat against the back of the cab,
learns again that the surest way out is through.

After Evensong

In the emptied church
the sanctuary lamp swings on its chains,
a body on an unanchored gibbet.
The new candle,
thwacked into place by the tired priest,
flickers.

I remember an evening surgery
in a sparsely furnished African hospital:
    the doctors, priests of the operating theatre,
    thump a newly-stitched uterus
    back into its abdominal cavity,
    the uterus, mute, still purple
    from giving birth to an infant
    who waits somewhere alone
    far from the form of his anaesthetized mother.
    The doctors stitch and chat.

All the while, the westering sun slides lower,
a pendant of fire outside the window.

Infant's Hands

Red as crabs
with thin rinds of fingernail
that scratch without hurting.
Fists clench,
are almost always tightly closed.

Do we enter life angry
to have left purple sleep
to fall into thin air,
loud light,
sharp noise?

One sound burst,
and rubber-band arms jerk,
fists fly open.
One instant flash of palm,
and the big, clanging world rushes in.

First of Winter

Wrists glowering from last winter's coat,
my son knots himself against the car door.
I drive; I am not responsible
for fall's jolt into winter.
—Or am I?

As the car hovers at the ice-slicked turn in the school drive
I acknowledge I carried him to birth
on this planet where farmers' fields sometimes freeze
under quilted, early snow.

Unbroken, the drifted eastern horizon
is just beginning to glow with the year's first winter dawn.

Although he is grumpy about his old coat,
I would give my twelve-year-old
this clean horizon whenever he wants it
for the rest of his life.
I would grant him broad fields,
clumps of tangled brambles, mosquito bogs,
yes, even sudden season changes.

But time is short.
The clock's minute digit flicks closer to the hour.
My son hauls his saxophone out of the back seat,
slams the door, hunches his shoulders into the cold,
and enters adolescence.

Venus's Voyage

Invisible to the naked eye, Venus
    crossed the face
    of the sun yesterday,
a dangerous journey
    she undertakes every day,
    except Earth is not in line for us to see.

How fragile and utterly beautiful
    the news pictures showed her
    as she followed her accustomed arc
between us and the sun,
    Milo's graceful goddess placing
    her bare foot among stars.

My teenage daughter sparked
    into wonder for an instant
    from her sullen mope,
a seventeen-year-old wanting
    to go somewhere, anywhere,
    as long as it's not here.

I also paused, caught by awe
    between trips to stove,
    refrigerator, table,
preparing dinner to feed, again,
    children who will grow up
    and travel away from me.

Upon Leaving a Daughter at College in Boston

Waiting for the tram before dawn,
      I taste the smoke
of a stranger's first cigarette;
      it becomes for me
a farewell offering scented
      sweet by tobacco,
darling of earth and water
      offered into air by fire,
the four elements complete,
      redolent
of all it took to build these dwellings,
      dark and somnolent,
these stores and restaurants,
      neon signs muted
by the hint of first light.

They were all made by labor of people
      such as these
waiting for the day's
      first tram,
shielding their privacy like
      precious flame
inside jackets and hunched shoulders,
      inside eyes
turned away from each other.
      Some lean
against posts or the big tram map;
      several sit

on the metal transit authority bench;
    one smokes;
an elderly Chinese woman walks past;
    soon her friend arrives.
They exchange gossip in syllables
    that float back,
incomprehensible to me.

Their conversation continues on the tram.
    The rest of us sit,
slowly working through
    the waking process,
dozing, reading, staring
    at lacquered reflections
obscured by fleeting streaks
    of light.

As the tram passes the street
    where you sleep
in your new bed, I gather the memory
    of early cigarette smoke
as if cupping my hands;
    I call upon
the blessings of all the souls
    in the tram:
the Chinese friends, the workers,
    weary or hopeful,
the smoker, the Black man
    dozing opposite me.
I can touch them no more than
    I can touch you,
who have my blood flowing
    in your veins.
I flatten my palm against the glass
    in farewell
as we pass your dormitory
    and mouth goodbye

as the tram sinks
        into its tunnel
under the Charles,
        curves down
the steely rails
        that rise behind us
and disappear
        like smoke.

Visiting Colonial Virginia

A Black man sits on the steps
        of a narrow brick house
older than my grandparents'
        generations in this land.
Their family lines crept across Europe
        to the ocean, then stopped
while this man's enslaved ancestors,
        laid brick, perhaps,
in this territory appropriated
        from the Powhatans.

The stoop behind the man is scalloped
        by the stepping and stepping,
passing and passing of feet,
        White, Black, Native American,
each grinding away a bit of stone
        as surely as the nearby river
bore away silt and soil
        before any of our forebears
gave it a name.

Today, I gaze through thick,
        tinted automobile glass
upon a place my family's eyes
        have not touched till now,
wondering who of my descendants
        will touch those other descendants,

and how much of us must be worn away,
    and by what rivers,
until hands meet
        across the great divide.

Alzheimer's Jonah

(at the nursing home)

Doctors, nurses, stewardesses
       and other official personnel
       shout instructions in my presence.
       Have they forgotten who I am?
Before some whale
       whose insides I can't recall
       belched me onto these shores,
       I was among the chosen.
These inhabitants,
       none from the land I remember,
       scurry about, grab at my elbows,
       loudly beg my pardon.
If only I could find a place
       away from their annoying repentance,
       maybe I could piece together the shreds
       of my orthodoxy and my ticket.
Then I would open a door
       and enter. On the other side—
       sounds of Hebrew,
       aroma of baking bread,
and home.

Fighting Fire

Haze settles like wrong into the clefts
        and hollows of the land.
I look up at the reddening sun, knowing
        not far away fire fighters
struggle in thin and scorching air
        to outwit devouring flames.
My father once manned a fire tower, from
        his nest of steel and glass
mapped lightning strikes, made calls,
        and directed armies
of men, mules, and planes to strategic sites.

        Now his body labors
to believe its own life. I pray for those
        watching the hot spots,
for the monitors, buzzers, and warning
        lights that do their work
as nurses go their rounds,
        tuck patients in,
and dim the lights into a half-darkness
        that settles uneasily
on those who die and those
        who merely sleep.

Farewelling Randy

For his wife, Bonnie

Quiet burdens their eardrums
when the beeping machines stop
tracking the weakening thrums
of his staggering heart.

With sobs, endearing words,
bars of favorite hymns he'd sung,
they ease him from the cords
that held him bound.

Released from life support,
they hold him, brush hair away from his eyes,
kiss where the surgeries hurt,
and say goodbye.

Rebecca at the End

For Rebecca Phillips

I drove home
        while your body waited
tethered by a pump
        to oxygen you would not breathe,
a tube into the nose
        for food you would not eat.
I planned to visit again,
        to hold your hand,
speak into your ear,
        hum another lullaby . . .

Heading home,
        traffic was sticky and slow,
Friday afternoon rush
        to get out,
out of the office, the city,
        cars backed up
for a block before the turn
        onto the highway,
thoughtful drivers sometimes slowing
        to let another into the creeping line . . .

Sometimes you just have to
        inch forward,

hope someone
      will see,
stop the whole works
         and let you go.

The Renaming of Jacob

For those dying alone

For you, doomed to act out
        in solitary struggle
        the drama of us all,
who, wrestling to the end,
        feel the opponent strain,
        who feel him almost fall,
who, locked arm to arm
        and thigh to thigh, will go
        the final match that is no game:
when, defeated, you lie gasping,
        may the opponent turn again
        and call you by your name.

The Great Vigil

On the evening of
        the Great Vigil
the sun set at the end
        of our street,
and the neighborhood
        went up in flame.

As I walked the dog into
        the conflagration,
I was busy thinking
        of my daughter,
pale with her white tee shirt
        and red hair,
standing candle-like beside
        our old friend's bed,
orange sun blazing behind her.
        Our friend turned
his eyes from death just once
        to recognize her,
but not to remember her name.
        Perhaps he saw her
as the taper lighting new fire
        in that dim place
he was about to traverse.

        The sun set.
The dog and I turned back,
        chill creeping
up our legs as we passed
        through
a community of cinders
        while my daughter,
tears glistening in the first headlights,
        drove home.

Thomas Merton

Thomas, you never could hold silent.
Dam your poetry,
and words will out in other ways.
Hermitage your voice,
and rocks and hills shout the glory so loudly
you must die or join in.
The fasts of quiet and prayer,
watch and labor
have hollowed your soul.
It waits bell-like
until wind strike,
and you ring clear.

The Wake

As sun creeps up,
the silo's black shadow
creeps down the dark barn roof
leaving a nimbus of frost,
a kind of wake,
where crystals melt,
folding into the rime below
until the effect is gone.
Those who have not seen it
may doubt my telling
of the moment
when white curls
into water,
then passes on.

Thief in the Night

"The day of the Lord will come like a thief in the night." 1 Thess 5:2

Break into my house, O welcome Thief.
Befriend the watchdog, force the door;
shatter the window, curtained in grief
when Vanity entered and spoiled my store.

Pass over my silver, tarnished, gray,
my golden ore not yet refined:
these trinkets and baubles cannot repay
your blood on entry, Thief most kind.

Steal into the room where sodden, asleep,
a jug of indulgence drained at my side,
I snore on fashionable clothing I keep
to use for a pillow, cushioning pride.

The shabbiest thing, I beg you, take:
myself—captive, sorrowful
dupe of my willful, vain mistake—
Sweet Thief, break in, and steal my soul!

Repentance

Regret's felled ash trunks
        must be buried
in pure, spring-fed waters,
        cradled,
laved, sung to
        by the spirit:
a sweet, long curing
        before the return for withes.

This is how
        to pull the bark,
to cut the splints
        that curl around your hand,
to weave your pliable life
        into something useful
for carrying fruit or nuts,
        for gathering eggs
to feed a family,
        for toting the newborn
when you move
        to a better place.

Germination

It seems there is nothing more
to say about these fields,
neatly combed,
seeds asleep under moist earth.

Poets and philosophers have said it all,
have meditated on field mice
and the destiny of man.

Farmers have said it all,
pausing their pickups mid-road to swap news
about the back forty,
the price of seed,
the likelihood of rain.

It has all been said.

The fields hold their peace
in varying shades of brown
under the wide, unpredictable sky.

The food of civilizations rests
beneath the hull of these fields
about which little more is being said.

Moving On

Above Lumberton with Judy

Elevation 6,870 ft.

We sprawled in the lee
of the ridgetop

Beneath our elbows,
thick duff, dried leaves:
former forest remains

Below,
scarred slopes,
mute stumps,
mute everything

The silence heavy,
sacred

On the knife-edged breeze
a hint of spice,
new-growth juniper
bruised by our passage

We slipped white-bread
baloney sandwiches
from baggies,
shared a canteen of cold water,
relished an apple each

Enough
just to be
above it all
where breath and companionship
were all that mattered

The Morada

(At an old penitente cemetery in New Mexico)

This is not a place of rottenness anymore.
The penitentes, now only five old men,
are too infirm to come here.
Instead, they go once a year to their chapel
near the arroyo. Its cement walls
thick like a mausoleum do not dampen
the howls, wails and yapping of these coyote men.

The church no longer comes
with its threatening chants, its plaster
statues said to drip tears and blood,
its wooden crosses from which the penitentes hung,
its mingled grief and guilt that plaited whips
of rough hemp and stones
so that every stripe bit tiny grooves
into sweating flesh, mingling salt and blood
in a stinging frenzy that made coyotes slink and hide.

The Morada is clean now,
swept dry by the wind of the alto plano
that soughs through the needles of the pines
planted at the corners and makes little flakes
of the whitewash that once painted
the markers. The flakes skip across sand

with a prickling sound like stars that prick the skies at night,
stars that make coyotes howl
and play-fight among themselves.

The dead are long gone from the Morada. The pickets
that once enclosed their graves point all directions
on the ground. Those left standing are askew
like doors of houses in ghost towns open
for no one—or anyone—to enter. The dead have gone on
and left this place to wind and stars.
They have left it to poets and lovers
who spread their jackets on the scant duff
and moan more quietly than the penitentes,
intone more humbly than the church,
sleep more lightly than the dead.

The coyote stops mid-lope to regard them
with yellow eyes, then continues on.

At the River Crescent

Humidity rises from evening earth
warm, rich and dark
as the loins of our parents
who, whatever their faults,
gave us life
to return to this spot where
tree toads, peepers,
crickets and cicadas
bless with their singing,
and the whippoorwill reminds:
      nothing
is more important than now.

Gravity

Springs squeak

the sound of weight
pulled toward earth's iron core
attracted by sun's seething mass

the slightest sigh
from this old mattress
as you shift in sleep
speaks a universe

I think I smell stars in your hair

House Blessing

Flashing lights warn me to the left:
> Oversize Load.

Half of someone's house
is rolling down the highway.
I bless it as I pass:
> May your future be
> better than your grammar.

Yet, grammar is a human thing;
it lives in our mouths,
chops words for the convenience
of pronouncing them,
breaks rules, makes new ones.
> When you meet your other half
> may you fit together perfectly.

Verb and noun, hand in glove,
spouse and spouse and children,
all the truncated parsings of existence:
> May we meet each other, touch, bond,
> find ourselves completed souls.

Attuned

A tuned thought
tightened to a single pitch
sounds through entire Earth.
We know it when it vibrates sympathetically
or when wrong jangles against it.

Such clear and perfect tones are sent
by pilgrims wizened on mountain tops,
cooks bent over generous stews,
children inspired at play,
or on the wings of chance remarks.

Constellations hear the harmony
of those fierce and gentle thoughts
while in the distant hills a shadow-black dog
gathers all their music in his throat,
bays stars and babies to their births.

Mardi Gras in Wisconsin

So this is Fat Tuesday,
        no aroma of sausage
            or bacon,
        no crowds madly courting
            tomorrow's hangover,

just busy people
        hurrying to lean work
            for meager wages
and me,
        driving inside the lines
            with the others,

but remembering King Cake
        and parades
            and hoping that
somewhere a baby drowses
        fattening
            on his mother's
                sweet milk.

Cloudburst

Windshield wipers pull a veil
        of rain across my view;
tree limbs' dark ink bleeds
        on vision's periphery;
in running water, headlights
        glisten and ripple.

I am sorry for pedestrians
        caught unprepared;
this downpour will sting
        their skin, deafen them.

Jaw and knuckles tight, I maneuver
        slippery streets
twisting up toward the house
        on the hill where
the old woman dozes in her rocker,
        and the baby,
lulled by the drumming,
        sucks her thumb and sleeps.

Thaw

All the water runs down
        the hill past our house, down
the hill from the cemetery
        where the dead lie
under their stones
        and the melting snow
drips, trickles, rushes.

        It's a laughing
stream by the time
        it reaches our house,
rich, dark snowwater flecked
        white with bubbles,
twisting and chuckling
        along the curbstones.

Morning, noon and night
        we hear the voice
of the water, like
        the warbling of birds, like
the voices of children
        running and skipping
from the city cemetery
        to houses
at the bottom of the hill.

Persephone's Return

Budded lilac lavenders the hedgerows,
purples white garages and red barns,
promises its perfume to tomorrow.
Everywhere, tiny, petaled throats are poised
to breathe fragrance into pallid spring.

Their breath, like Hade's reprieve,
will bring color to Demeter's cheeks,
warmth to her lips,
will swell ice-locked streams
into rills of laughter.

Just a Sprig of Lilac

A body could brighten up this place
with a sprig—just a single sprig
could freshen up, could liven up,
could cheer up the damask tablecloth,
the hand-done antimacassars,
the proper, straight-backed chairs.

A body could bring a touch of color
to this white and walnut room
with just a sprig of lilac in a glass.

Double in White

Inside thick stairwell glass
my reflection rises
through pear trees.
Blossoms load
their twigs and branches,
puffs of white circlets
garlanding every stem.

At each landing I stop,
allow my alter-self
to savor the sensation
of being touched, caressed
by confetti of trembling white.
At each interior turn I lose her,
then find her again,
hair, arms, body
aglow with tiny rounds of sun
through paper-thin petals.

Wreathed in white,
twined, twinned,
I climb and climb,
spiraling upward,
wanting her to never end.

Eucharist in Ashland, Wisconsin

Water hisses on the shoal at the point, slaps,
recalls the shipwrecks that dot these shores
as surely as towns dot the map.

From the point gazebo, I gaze past the oredocks,
past other spits of land to where slate water
blends into slate sky: a true November lakescape

where empty deciduous trees fur the lakeshore
in charcoal broken by black-green pine
or yellow late aspen and tamarack.

Behind me, in Picasso blue, towers the idle
Marine Travel Lift; its canvas and metal truss
swings, creaks in the windgusts.

Yachts, taped and lashed, sit on the pier,
resemble shrouded, long-snouted pigs,
fat bellies supported by blocks.

Later, in the cavernous Episcopal church,
long and ribbed with dark wood like the hull
of an overturned Viking vessel,

the congregation's songs are lost. Sound waves
slide around piers and columns to reach the end
of the apse, but forget to return to our straining ears.

The priest, young with dark eyes, speaks of God's mark
sealed onto our foreheads in holy chrism, an invisible
cable to reel us in, moor us to Heaven. Flung

by his diocese to the tip of this peninsula, he raises
the elements as generations of priests have done.
His arms fill with the shape of the land.

Minaret

Needle
of sound
as thin
as the tower
from which it comes

descends in pitch,
gathers fullness, throat,
calls the righteous to form,
the devout to prayer.

Ululations of vocals lightly
differentiated by consonants:

the human spirit held high,
quivering, brilliant, vulnerable;
human suffering, holy joy
bound together,
edges blurred:
supplication, song.

Girl and Truck

Semi's wheels mesmerize
the child in the car's back seat.
Her eyes gaze into epicenters
of blasts that buffet the car.

At eye level, the wheels seem to pause
and spin backward just for her.

Then, as the truck pulls ahead,
they slow and spin forward once more:

a sign, a gesture, a wink
from a behemoth of the road
to one who holds the future
in her cells.

Writer

Beside the river she walks
        searching for words bright and balanced,
        riverstones to jangle in her pockets,
        to finger over and again.

She is a stone,
        shepherd's ammunition
        chosen, stored
        to hurtle from the sling
        into some Goliath.

Smooth-worn word,
        she will sink in,
        plant him in earth.

When in Your Garden Poets Recite

you will not regret
stacked dinner dishes
corks rolled under shrubs

there will be midnight strolls
to savor the nonsound
of a town asleep

out of the dark
the pink of an upturned palm
will call you on

you will walk on water
gaze through ice
into black depths and shiver

steamships' throaty whistles
will clang your heart against
the wide horizon the open sea

leaves of your grape arbor
will caress each other
in the breath of words

and wine from that year
will be burgundy purple
with an aroma no one can name

Runner I

He runs as if he and
air are one,
his body merely
an occasion
for their ecstatic union.

Now I understand what
we were made for:
a fierce abandonment,
a dedication,
a mind, an eye
fixed on the end.

The starter's gun
salutes
the first sharp intake of
breath,
the finish tape flies apart
in joy,

let everything else
blur by.

My Life as a Bullet

I remember heat
from being forged,
then fitting neatly
with my companions
inside a dark box.

Then a flash of light,
the waiting chamber,
a jostle
and a click.

I found my vocation
with the explosion,
the long, grooved shaft
spinning me, heating me,
giving me my own
special song,

then the burst of light,
the friction of air's
little claws,
then impact
misshaping my hot metal,
a tearing,
a splintering . . .

then slowing,
burying myself deep
to become part of
someone else's story.

For me, it was a good life;
I did what I was made to do.

Can you say as much
for yourself?

Runner II

For St. Paul

She presses toward the end,
                waiting.
Her goal: to slice the passing blur
so cleanly not a hair will catch or snag.
Though the gliding crowd swells its roar,
her ears are tuned to only one rhythm:
legs, lungs, heart pumping together.

Then
            ribs rise,
chest fills to snap the homing tape.
The stadium slows,
shudders to a halt;
the rhythm resolves
into voices' thunder.

            She has done it.
            She has won it.
She held, and reached the other side!

Lone Skateboarder

He strops and strops
the jump,
curling to momentum's apex
then hanging an instant
before gravity's undertow
sucks him back down.

In this maddening repetition
of hard rubber wheels,
I imagine he feels
the knuckling drive of concrete,
wood's smooth peel.
He tests tension
in calves and thighs,
adjusts pressure
on the soles of his feet,
bends his waist,
lifts his arms.

Alone,
under the locust-sizzling sun,
he'll make the jump.
I hope to look up
from my papers
and see him
mid-air,
arms poised,

set free.

Baltimore Oriole

It is a splash of orange
under my neighbor's plum tree
and a song so swift it is gone
before I pull the binoculars from their case.

This should not be surprising
in a world where children's commotion and laughter
ripple through the pool of my solitude
such a short time before moving on

or where the picture I held last night of my father
made me catch my breath,
amazed that someone so recently young
could turn old and be no more.

This is not a poem about grief;
it is about joy, timeless yet fleeting
like a bright thread running through a tapestry,
appearing, disappearing, stitching my days together

with orange on its wings.

Fountain

So many jets of water
laughing white
tossing themselves to the sky
Ha-Ha!
utterly confident of coming
down in just the right spot

To be that free to fling myself
for the zenith
for the shape of the arc
that exists
only when nothing else matters

to fall

into that long kiss with gravity
into liquid applause
Splash!
foam shoulders gleam
pale for an instant
then disappear to do it
all over again

Hopscotch

It started with a chunk of gypsum
so soft
it gave itself away
every time we pressed it
onto rough sidewalk.

How like my own body,
softening now with age,
thin hair streaked—
white lines not as bold
as the ones we drew.

My pen is still busy, busy
drawing lines and loops,
outlining space
into lopsided boxes,
designing impossible leaps.

I take my stub of chalk,
builders' detritus,
throw it beyond the edge
of my own creation,
tuck my leg,
                begin.

Fly Fishing

An oncoming car's wheel slogs
        into a pothole.
Through already descending lashes
        I see the water come,
white, wave-shaped, leaping
        in an arc
toward its rapping impact
        with my windshield
and my involuntary blink.
        That poised moment
when the arc is still intact
        and water knows nothing
of obstacles, catches at my throat,

        reminds me
of baseball when the batter
        plans to bunt.
Pitcher, shortstop, basemen
        move forward
as the ball leaves
        the pitcher's hand.
All, intent, unknow
        everything
except the impact of wood
        on whitened leather.

I have seen a bird fall
    mid-flight,
a holy man greet death
    with shining eyes,
my child lift her foot
    for her first step.
I have gazed into memory-erasing
    blue, waiting
for sky to birth
    its first star.

It is this throw, this cast
    of all change,
like a line curling
    above a river,
extending, descending,
    that makes me rise,
forgetting all,
    to put my mouth
around the meeting of the worlds.

Lumberton is a real town in an area historically denuded by clearcut logging where the abused spirit of the land pervaded both place and people. The poems in this book explore various kinds of abuse and spiritual impoverishment as well as growth of awareness and healing. The journey from desolation toward wholeness proceeds in ordinary ways: waiting quietly like a bare field under a wide sky, noticing the budding lilac, or simply taking the next first step. We can leave our Lumbertons.

Sheryl Slocum is the ESL Coordinator at Alverno College in Milwaukee. She is a member of the Hartford Avenue Poets and of the Wisconsin Fellowship of Poets.

www.ingramcontent.com/pod-product-compliance
Lightning Source LLC
Chambersburg PA
CBHW061952070426
42450CB00007BA/1326